Cell Church Stories as Signs of Mission

Bob Hopkins (editor)
Coordinator, Anglican Church Planting Initiatives
and NSM Curate, St Thomas, Crookes, Sheffield

Roy Hollands CA
Church Army Parish Evangelist, The Holy Apostles, Leicester

Karen Hamblin
Director of Youth and Children's Work, St Alkmund's, Derby

Phil Pawley
Director of Mission, St Mark's, Haydock, Merseyside
and Evangelism Team Leader, Liverpool Diocese

Kerry Thorpe
Senior Minister, Harvest New Anglican Church, Margate

GROVE BOOKS LIMITED
RIDLEY HALL RD CAMBRIDGE CB3 9HU

Contents

1. Introduction and Background to Cell Church 3

2. A UPA Church Plant from Holy Apostles, Leicester 9

3. Youth Cells at St Alkmund's, Derby 14

4. 'Big Bang' Transition at St Mark's, Haydock 19

5. Transition and Transplant—'Harvest,' Margate 24

Acknowledgements

I thank my wife, Mary, who has repeatedly brought a prophetic reminder of how important cell principles are for future mission. Thanks also to past members of our team at ACPI, Richard White and Jon Fox who have re-enforced this and helped us develop these ideas. And not least to the authors of the four stories here, together with their churches and many others who have had the faith and courage to pioneer such adventurous initiatives.

The Cover Illustration is by Peter Ashton

Church Army and the Grove Evangelism Series

Church Army has over 350 evangelists working in five areas of focus, at the cutting edge of evangelism in the UK. It co-sponsors the publication of the Grove Evangelism Series as part of its aim of stimulating discussion about evangelism strategies, and sharing its experience of front-line evangelism.

Further details about Church Army are available from:
Church Army, Independents Road, Blackheath, London SE3 9LG.
Telephone: 020 8318 1226. Fax: 020 8318 5258.
Registered charity number: 226226

First Impression August 2000
ISSN 1367-0840
ISBN 1 85174 440 1

1
Introduction and Background to Cell Church
Bob Hopkins

This booklet explores cell church for today in Europe, largely through the telling of four recent stories. Each shows the implementation of cell principles in very different ways and in very different situations. I could have focused on early pioneers like Howard Astin[1] and Martin Garner,[2] but these stories have already been written. I want to introduce these stories with a brief explanation of what cell church is and where I see it meeting today's challenges.

Putting Cell Church in its Place
Some see cell church as a church growth technique. Others assess it as a model of church from third world cultures which is of little significance in the (supposedly) post-Christian West. Yet others seem to get so mesmerized by the 'New Paradigm' that they adopt it lock, stock and barrel. We hear stories of ever larger 'mega' cell churches. First Korea, then Nigeria and now Columbia and the 'G12' model with thousands of people. However, my interest is to identify the underlying mission principles in the model so that we can decide where it fits in our plural Western cultures and what adaptations are needed.

So What is All the Fuss About?
Cell church is more radical than just a new approach to home groups.[3] Ralph Neighbour believes that for those conditioned by Western, congregational models of church the concept can be so foreign that he refuses to teach on it for anything less than a week! His book,[4] seminars and materials first popularized cell church although I consider David Prior described the same principles a decade earlier.[5]
Perhaps the simplest way to show the contrast is with a diagram given by Ian Freestone,[6] reproduced in figure 1 overleaf. We can summarize the essence of cell church as a) the small group is seen as fully church; b) outreach

1 Howard Astin, *Body and Cell* (Monarch CPAS, 1998).
2 George Lings, 'Has Church reached its Cell Buy Date?' in *Encounters on the Edge* No 3 (1999).
3 See also my introduction for those new to cell church, *Explaining Cell Church*, Bob Hopkins (Administry Mini-Guide 12, 1998).
4 Ralph Neighbour, *Where Do We Go From Here?* (Touch Publications, 1990).
5 David Prior, *The Church in the Home* (Marshalls, 1983).
6 Ian Freestone, *A New Way of being Church* (ACPI,1995).

is principally from a welcoming small group, and c) all the ministry of the church happens through the cells rather than in programs at the congregational level. Building on this, there are other typical marks of cell church: small groups aim to multiply; cell leaders are supported and equipped; small is believed to be good; there is movement from house to house; new leaders are grown by apprenticeship; discipleship concerns lifestyle ; small groups seek real community.

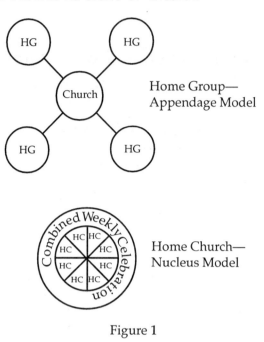

Home Group—
Appendage Model

Home Church—
Nucleus Model

Figure 1

It helps to dispel misunderstandings to say what cell church is not. Firstly it does *not* mean no service on Sunday in the parish church. Because this system emphasizes cell *and* celebration, Sunday is the overflow of the cell life and to the visitor will not seem that different from many other services. They may pick up that small groups are particularly important and create a special sense of community, with one cell doing the welcome, one leading prayers and another sharing testimony. Otherwise it need not be an un-Anglican Sunday experience.

Another common misunderstanding is that because cell is fully church, you have to do everything that is essential to church at that level—sacraments included. Some may take that view but most do not, considering it is no less church because certain things are best done in a large group, whilst others fit much better in a small group context. Baptisms may be done in the large Sunday gathering of all cells, but the convert's cell leader baptizes together with the vicar/minister. Eucharist may be for Sunday celebrations but the different belonging of a shared meal is possible in cell-sized small groups and *Alpha* has shown the gospel power of that.

Lastly, although in classic cell church everyone is in a small group, the model does not depend on this and it is perfectly possible for the structures that support and pastor cell members to also provide for church members not yet in cells, and even non-attending parishioners.

Latest Fashion or a Vital Mission Strategy for 21ˢᵗ Century?
I am concerned that every few years a wave of interest in the latest New Thing sweeps through the Western church. From church planting, to Willow-Creek seeker services, to purpose-driven churches, to *Alpha*, to cell church, to... Some leaders, influenced perhaps by the prevailing consumerist environment or driven by a desperate need to reverse decline, may jump from one to the other. This will make their congregations seasick, risk disillusionment and certainly not take us further in our task of mission and evangelism. It seems to me that these waves emerge because someone has discovered a really crucial principle by prayer and hard work, and applied it successfully in their context. We must look past their model or package to the underlying principles and then assess the suitability for our own context and adapt appropriately.

Our four stories show how cell principles are being applied and adapted, not as a blueprint or fixed package, but in creative tension with their context. But first I choose three analytical frameworks to help us put cell church in its place as having a particularly crucial contribution for evangelism and mission today.

A Historic and Geographical Framework
Christianity in the first three centuries started as a Jewish sect and evolved into a radical mission movement in a setting of polytheism and Greek philosophy. The success of the movement was bottom up, from the grass roots. Though persecuted and marginalized its effectiveness led ultimately to a transformation of the Roman Empire.[7] The result was Christendom, a society with an established church, and worldview and values based on the Judeo-Christian story and principles. This sustained itself for some sixteen centuries, and extended itself over different continents with varying effectiveness. However, in Western Europe it has now been progressively eroded, creating a completely new situation. The institutional church is left as a very thin 'crust' floating on a rapidly changing sea of pluralism and secularism in a society loosely basing itself on a worldview centred on the the free market economy and with a host of competing value systems.

Of utmost importance is the recognition that this context is not static but rapidly changing. Though broadly 'post-Christendom' there are still elements of Christendom around as well as some communities that are effectively pre-Christian and others reactively post-Christian. Figure 2 overleaf represents this very simplified scheme and complements the analysis of Paul Simmonds.[8]

7 See Rodney Stark, *The Rise of Christianity* (Harper Collins, 1997).
8 Paul Simmonds, *From Maintenance to Mission* (Grove Evangelism booklet Ev 32) p 5.

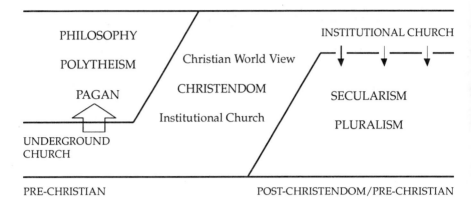

PHILOSOPHY

POLYTHEISM   Christian World View

PAGAN   CHRISTENDOM

                    Institutional Church

UNDERGROUND
CHURCH

INSTITUTIONAL CHURCH

SECULARISM

PLURALISM

PRE-CHRISTIAN   POST-CHRISTENDOM/PRE-CHRISTIAN

Figure 2

My contention is that it is very hard to re-evangelize our nation with a top-down approach from the thin crust of institutional Christianity. Rather, we shall require a radical new model of church, akin to the first three centuries, if it is to be earthed in (say) estates where Jesus and the biblical story are wholly unknown. Cell church may be just such a model. It may therefore be much more significant that the cultures from which it has come to us are pre-Christian than that they are Asian or African.

A Church and Mission Framework

Figure 3 is another simplified attempt to represent the situation (it was written up more fully elsewhere[9]). It shows active church as some 5–15% of the population—tending to come from the older generation. Related to this is a reducing fringe of folk with some regular points of contact. Until a decade or so ago, some parish consultants recommended that the churches' task of evangelism should focus on draw-

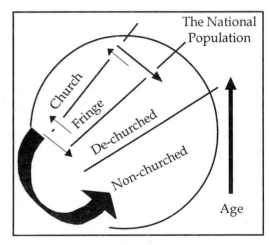

The National Population

Church

Fringe

De-churched

Non-churched

Age

Figure 3

9   Bob Hopkins, *News from Anglican Church Planting Initiatives*, No 3 (ACPI, 1997).

6

ing this fringe back into active membership—a big enough task for any church. However, church planting and seeker-sensitive church have challenged us to move beyond the fringe to what was termed the unchurched. Such mission experience is showing that beyond the fringe are those who once were involved with church and dropped out at different points for a host of reasons. These are better described as the de-churched and often have stronger more traditional opinions about how church should be than attendees. The challenge remains to reach the truly non-churched among the youth, urban estates and ethnic minorities. The diagram shows that, although church planting and seeker services change the direction of evangelism from in-drag to outreach, they still start with church as we know it and either re-locate it or take bits out of it that may put off non-attenders. To reach the non-churched we must 'stop starting with the church,' come outside the circle and re-imagine church by a process of engagement, evangelism and mission among them and allowing them to develop different forms of church appropriate to their many contexts.

Cell church is very significant here in that it arises from small discipleship-based faith communities which can be incarnational. This smaller building block can also be much more socially flexible, able to relate to a wider range of contexts than congregations with all their 'taboos.' Our emerging cultures are seeking belonging and community and cell meets this need and provides a way of being church that can build on group-based evangelism such as *Alpha* and *Emmaus*.

A Church/Discipleship Framework

Many find Bill Beckham's book on cell church the most illuminating.[10] He does a historical analysis from the perspective of the church as 'two winged' with cell- and celebration-sized expressions. This follows the disciples gathering in homes and temple courts (Act 2.42f and elsewhere). He believes that Constantine's legalization of Christianity in the fourth century, resulted in the formalization of church into the single 'wing' of large institutional celebration gatherings only. With brief exceptions through history he attributes the weakness of the Christendom model to this unbalanced bird, unable to properly fulfil its calling and 'fly'!

But this analysis not only reads back too many ills of the church to Constantine, it also begs the question of how a 'grounded' Christendom survived for sixteen centuries! This reflection led me to the theory that Christendom was not in fact one-winged for much of its history. The small group discipleship 'wing' continued to exist but was simply not called church. The task of worship, fellowship, teaching and evangelizing the next generation

---

10   William A Beckham, *The Second Reformation* (Touch Publications, 1995).

happened in homes in *extended* Christian families. In parts of society where this structure weakened, Christians pioneered a small group discipling system called 'schools' to form the next generation in the biblical story and Christian values.

If we free ourselves from the erroneous assumption that church is primarily defined by form and structure and focus on the greater importance of function instead, we might define church as 'a Jesus community of disciple-making disciples.' The degradation of Christendom is due to the loss of this function, much more effectively performed over the generations by extended Christian family and Christian schools than by what we called church—a Sunday event in a religious building. Our crisis and the need to rediscover the heart of mission for re-evangelization of our nation is due to the loss of extended family, the breakdown of nuclear family and the loss of Christian schools. The function of these in discipleship and formation of a Christian worldview and values is our challenge in the 21st century and this can be restored by cell church (among other models).

Conclusion

It is harder to recover a Christian worldview and values than maintain them and it requires new models. Hence our overwhelming need for evangelism and mission based on a small group discipleship model which then continues as the model of church (as with *Alpha* and *Alpha* follow-up). There *are* different cultures in Asia and Africa where cell church thrives but the important thing is what we now have in common with these continents, not what is distinct. In much of our country and continent we share a pre-Christian setting and, as Robert Warren has so rightly described,[11] only a missionary-centred church rather than a maintenance-centred model will deliver.

---

11   Robert Warren, *Building Missionary Congregations* (Church House Publishing, 1997).

2

A UPA Church Plant from Holy Apostles, Leicester

Roy Hollands CA

Planting a new church from scratch, starting with a single cell, perhaps offers the most straightforward option to explore cell church principles. There are few issues to do with making the transition and one can grow into each stage of developing a cell-based system. It also has great advantages for church planting as resources are not tied up too soon in a building and a Sunday event. Rather the emphasis can be on serving the neighbourhood, evangelism and the evolving of a truly indigenous community of faith. It models incarnation and is especially appropriate to non-churched, deprived urban estates where so easily outsiders can 'do church for them.' Some have suggested that the use of homes does not fit council estate hospitality which may be family centred. However, Roy and his team, again with the hallmark of adaptation rather than slavish copying, are generating an exciting non-book version of cell. Meetings have to be non-academic and flexible when there is TV football in the room and possible interruption by a police call. This case study also illustrates what is known as intergenerational cells, but again rather than impose a package they have applied the model to fit with local social patterns. As a plant their celebration has had to evolve and (interestingly) is still not weekly.

The plant is within the parish of The Church of The Holy Apostles in Leicester, population 12,402, electoral roll 138. The parish church itself was a plant from the neighbouring parish of The Church of The Martyrs in 1904, with the present building completed in 1924. There are roughly three identifiable areas of housing: late 19th-century terraces around the church building to the north, east and south; inter-war semi-detached further south; and various styles of inter-war council housing built in an estate to the west and further north. The council estate extends further than the parish boundary and roughly the other half of it is in the next deanery. The tradition of the parish has always been broadly low evangelical, with some charismatic elements. There are three services at the parish church on a Sunday: 9am Holy Communion (BCP and ASB); 10.30am Family Service; 6.30pm Evening Prayer or Holy Communion. The largest congregation is the 10.30 with around a hundred people, with each of the others being between ten to fifteen people. Attendance at 10.30 has remained stable for about the last six years, whilst the other two have slowly decreased for various reasons.

In the 1950s a classic mission hall, dedicated as St Oswald's, was planted on the council estate as part of a vision to raise a congregation there. This thrived in the 1970s but by the 90s had dwindled until it was closed in April

1997 at the request of the few remaining members. I was asked to research and write a report on the best way forward for this area and did so with the help of George Lings of Church Army's Sheffield Centre. I also read several books: Roland Allen's *Missionary Methods—St Paul's or Ours*; Paul Yonggi Cho's *Successful Home Cell Groups*; Ian Freestone's *A New Way of Being Church* and Grove Evangelism booklet Ev 22 about mission in local authority estates (LAEs). This study and my three years' experience of the area, made a cell model seem suited to renewing mission there for a number of reasons. St Oswald's building had been a target for vandalism and robbery, so meeting in houses seemed better than creating a new target. Local people have an immunity to the initiatives of institutions, so re-launching as 'your Parish Church' would not get under their skin. Learning from the persecuted church we felt called to be 'subversive' of local secular culture rather than openly challenging it. Cells also provide, perhaps most importantly, a structure to grow relatively quickly whilst also effectively discipling new Christians in a relational way which makes sense in the local 'non-book' culture.

A small home group already met on the estate, made up of five people, three of whom lived there. In the autumn of 1997 my wife, Ruth, and I joined this group and encouraged them to pray for the right way forward for a plant in the area. Eventually three of the group felt called to become the initial planting team, along with Ruth and myself. The other two members decided to move to a different house group. We were therefore left with a group of five, only one of whom did not live in the estate.

Building the Team

To build the team and help us understand the resources we brought to the planting process we worked through the Willow Creek *Network* course, designed to help new members work out how they can serve as part of an existing church. We used it to work out what kind of church we were to be, given that we were it. The results further clarified the general direction of subversive relational church planting working from our own homes. The team was made up of Ruth and me with two young children; Ruth Souter with two teenagers, one toddler and a part-time job; Shirley Letts with grown up children; and Ian Starie, single and unemployed. The main qualities we were looking for in members were: being an Anglican living locally in the estate; feeling a call to be part of the plant; having a desire to be imaginative in our efforts to demonstrate the Kingdom of God locally. In September 1998 we were commissioned by the parish to plant a new church in the area. We decided to call ourselves *LivingStones*, following a Bible study on 1 Peter 2.1–12.

From the beginning, meeting to pray has been an important part of our church life. Very soon we did not have time to do everything in one meeting so we arranged two meetings a week at times that suited us and that we also thought might suit people who would join us. We therefore developed a midweek meeting for prayer, starting at 11am with drinks and 'catching up' conversation followed by prayer for each other, for other people we were trying to bring to Christ and for the growth of the church and God's kingdom in the area. Most of us would then stay on to eat together, having brought a packed lunch. Our other meeting was on a Friday evening for learning and worship. Early on we looked into the resources provided by *Unlock*, then called *EUTP*, for churches in UPAs and LAEs. We decided to use their sessions on relationships, priorities and money called 'Go For It' which use scenes from the film *The Full Monty*. This attracted some interest in itself. As one neighbour put it: 'Bible studies on *The Full Monty*? I've got to see that!' We have found *Unlock*'s advice and recommendations invaluable in our efforts to bring the gospel to a 'non-book' culture.

First Growth

'Go For It' brought our first convert, Raj, a young man from a Sikh family we had known for a few years. One evening he told us that his father had asked him why he did not become a Christian since he spent so much time with Christians. Raj replied that he would if he knew how. When he told us we were only too pleased to explain it all to him and he has been a regular member of the church ever since. After the course using *The Full Monty* we developed our own learning sessions about the Ten Commandments using *Unlock*'s pattern.

During this period the mother of a family we had known for some years joined us for most Friday evenings, mainly because it got her out of the house while her husband had his friends round to watch wrestling. Nevertheless she gradually seemed to enjoy the meetings and to join in with some discussion. One evening she turned up with a black eye and other bruises which her cousin had caused. We were at a particularly quiet part of the meeting when there was a loud knock at the door. It was her husband who had come to bring her home because the police were there for a statement from her about the attack. In recent months the relationship with her husband has deteriorated. He sometimes makes it difficult for her to leave the house so we have not seen her much lately. As with many other people here there are so many urgent circumstances which make church seem like a luxury pastime to them.

By early 1999 we were growing in numbers and sense of purpose. Two couples had joined us from the Holy Apostles' congregation as they were from the estate and felt more at home with *LivingStones*. One couple, John and Dorinda, have two young boys, so we often had four children under five at our midweek prayer meetings. We encouraged them to pray with us

11

and they sometimes did, but we did not try to make them stay quiet while we prayed, we just prayed loudly over their loud games! As other people joined us meetings became quite crowded and we began to consider the process of multiplying, again with the help of George Lings. In June we became two cells, introducing monthly celebration meetings for the whole church. We also began a fortnightly cell-leaders' cell, which the parish vicar attends once a month. We named the two cells after the roads they usually meet on, Turville cell and Winstanley cell. Winstanley has four children so their worship and learning meeting is early on Saturday evenings after a shared tea which means that the children can be fully involved and still get to bed before they are too tired. Turville still meets on Friday evening, as they are mainly adults.

Teaching and Discipleship

Soon after multiplying we started the *Network* course again, to establish the new cells' identities and directions and to help the new people understand their roles. We have often postponed sessions when people are absent because of the frequent emergencies and irregular work patterns which are part of life here. Winstanley started doing *Network* with the involvement of the children, as they take part in everything else. This soon proved too difficult and time-consuming, so two people from Turville cell came on Saturdays to occupy the children while the adults followed *Network*. This is one example of how the cells work together and share resources at all times, not just for celebrations. Following a course of cumulative learning has, however, been very costly in time and effort and we have realized that the best way for people to learn in our situation is through regular fellowship and personal teaching as circumstances arise. The main teaching in the church is now at the monthly celebration, leaving cell meetings for personal 'edification,' encouragement and application of issues arising from the month's teaching. This is a more suitable mixture into which to welcome enquirers and new Christians. From reading D Michael Henderson's 'John Wesley's Class Meeting' we have learned the value of separating teaching events from fellowship and discipling meetings.

We have no special teaching for the children. As a reflection of the local culture, where adults and children do not normally do things separately, we aim for what we call 'whole family discipleship.' We encourage the parents in the church to teach their children Christianity at home and to encourage their children's participation in meetings and we emphasize the need for the whole family to pull together in following Jesus. The adults have needed to be ready to learn from the children too, as Jesus himself said we should!

We first heard about the 'four Ws' (Welcome, Worship, Word and Witness) at a conference in September 1999 and realized we were doing them all, but in two meetings a week, not one. At the Wednesday lunch time meetings we do 'Worship' and 'Witness,' especially in our intercessory prayers. Then at the weekend meeting we do 'Worship' and 'Word.' There is a 'Welcome' at both meetings, usually involving tea, joking and biscuits! We have frequently used ideas from Wild Goose's *Wee Worship Book* as well as the ASB and even the BCP (the Cathechism and suggested homilies, heavily adapted, are a good starter for basic teaching). Occasionally we also write or adapt our own liturgy, usually after the style of *Wee Worship*. Several members have written some good poetry which reflects much of our experience of God as individuals and as a group. Outreach is usually in the form of friendship and social contacts. Most cell members play an active part in the local community and this, along with the acceptability of church meetings in our own homes, has made our meetings attractive to several people we know. At Christmas Winstanley cell plans to go carol singing around all their 'fringe' people, giving out Christmas cards they made together.

Celebrations

The monthly celebrations after multiplying were in Ruth Souter's garden during the summer and we are now able to use the Roman Catholic Parish Hall in the centre of the estate. We have a very good 'practical ecumenism' going on with the Catholics as both churches share a similar understanding of mission and service for the local area. In August the celebration was a baptism service in Ruth's garden using a very large inflatable paddling pool to baptize Raj and another young man. An older local man also re-took his baptism vows. John Rainer, the vicar, joined us for this and did the baptisms. In October we celebrated our first Holy Communion as a church in the Catholic Parish Hall on a Sunday afternoon. November was a parish gift day in which *LivingStones* took part. Our December celebration was an evening of prayers and meditations on New Year's Eve, and we had a joint Christmas dinner and party on Christmas Day in the Catholic Hall.

The fortnightly leaders' cell has been vital in maintaining vision and unity. In addition the same group also meets roughly fortnightly to discuss the direction of the church and administrative matters. New cell leaders are emerging and attend all the leaders' meetings as part of their 'apprenticeship,' as well as helping lead their cell.

In September 1998 there were five adults and three children meeting as one cell. In December 1999 there are thirteen adults and six children meeting as two cells. We also now have a substantial 'fringe' of interested and acquainted people. We can see the vision for *LivingStones* developing as a growing community of Christians making the best of life on our estate and serving our area and the local people; living out God's Kingdom and offering hope to the great number of people who struggle with day-to-day life here.

3

Youth Cells at St Alkmund's, Derby

Karen Hamblin

This cameo not only describes how cell principles are being applied to church youth work but also illustrates that cell need not be a whole church strategy. The adult congregation considered and rejected the cell system, at least for now. The evangelism and mission advantages of cell are particularly relevant to our emerging cultures—hence it should be no surprise that youth work is the first area where many churches are finding cell principles appropriate. Over the past decade or so experience has led to the identification of the need of today's youth for belonging both to a small intimate peer group and to a large anonymous happening/crowd sized gathering. The cell and celebration system fits very well.

So, of the many churches exploring youth cells I chose Derby because they have hit a lot of the issues and are responding really creatively with a well thought out rationale. What is so encouraging in this and other similar stories, is the huge potential of youth to lead and the signs of the beginning of a generation of godly young people sold out for God. The expected evangelistic fruit has taken longer than hoped, maybe because there is a culture to break. Once again adaptation is the hallmark and the youth play a key role in shaping the strategy.

St Alkmund's is an Anglican church in Derby Diocese. The parish is located on the northern edge of the city, but has an eclectic congregation from across the city. It is evangelical/charismatic by tradition and the overall congregation numbers around 650, of which approximately 120 are under 18. Vision for the whole church is based around the 'Four Pillars' of growth through evangelism, every member in a small group, leadership development and training, and mercy ministries. These work out through the values of relating and creating (relationship with people and with Jesus), belonging, believing and behaving.

I have been the Director of Youth and Children's Work here for 6 years, working with a large, faithful and (it seems) ever-changing team of volunteers. In the last three years I have been joined by Andrew, a full time youth worker, who was employed to specifically work with 16–25 year olds.

Looking back I can see God's pattern emerging. Before 1997 there was a group of about 30 young people aged 14–18, meeting once a week after the Sunday evening service. We recognized the need for change as this group developed a consumer mentality, exhausting us as leaders and never satisfying them. In order to develop all our relationships we divided them into three groups, each with two adult leaders meeting in different rooms in the church. Things improved further when we moved out of the church into people's homes, creating a far more intimate atmosphere. We were then asked to pilot a course for Anglicans for Renewal called *Journey to the Eye of the Storm* (currently being revised). This encourages understanding and practical application of the work of the Holy Spirit and encourages youth to lead with adult mentoring. It worked brilliantly and opened our eyes to the advantages of peer leaders. At the time we were reading about cell and beginning to discuss the implications of this for the youth work. We realized that we were in fact only a few steps away from a cell-like structure, but lacked the philosophy that goes with it. This was the greatest adjustment for us.

With hindsight I can identify five major factors which moved us firmly in the direction of cell: a desire to see real discipleship and not just consumerism; a longing to see new young people saved and discipled; a knowledge that youth had more to give and the need to find the right vehicle; an urgent desire to stop the loss of youth from the church and to see prodigals return.

We implemented cell in September 1997. We felt that we had found something that might have the answers to some of our frustrations in that it would: build on the relational youth work already established; fly in the face of consumerism; create huge potential for evangelism and discipleship; allow young people's giftings to be used and developed in a safe environment.

At this time the concept of cell was being tentatively explored in the church, but subsequently the church leadership decided that it was not the right way forward for the church as a whole. Therefore we are not a cell church, nor are there any plans to become one and in order to avoid confusion our youth cells are called small groups rather than cells. However, the cell model was still seen as suitable for youth and so we continued to read around the subject, visit churches making the transition to cell church, talk with Paul Hopkins, YWAM's consultant on youth cells, and chew it over long and hard. We decided on a clean break and a new start for the 13–18 age band, tying in with the beginning of the new academic year.

Setting Up

The groups were set up as single-sex, peer-led groups with the full age range present in each. We identified group leaders through the *Journey to the Eye of the Storm* course that the youth had previously done. Most were 15–18 and we tried to avoid those with major exams that academic year.

We opted for single-sex groups because our youth had been through a bad patch of 'cattle market' mentality when relationships, with all their teenage angst, were the major feature of life. It was not, and still is not, a decision set in stone. The youth themselves now prefer single-sex groups, having begun them sceptically. They feel there is room for greater openness and an easier atmosphere in which to discuss things. I think it also makes it easier for peer leaders who may not have the maturity to handle difficult relation-ship issues. However, groups mix freely through Friday evening outreach, Sunday evening service and things that they organize spontaneously, so there is no sense of separation.

Small groups meet weekly, in church members' homes, on Sunday after-noons and then come together to the evening service. We currently have six small groups, two female and four male. Each has a core attendance of five to six, with up to eight on each group's list. Once a month we come together as a youth congregation (called *Wired*) to celebrate small group life. All the groups contribute and have major input in shaping and leading this time.

Leadership

We made mistakes initially in the choice of some of our leaders. Moving from a programme-based model to a value-driven one was harder than we had anticipated, for all of us. One of the girl's groups had to be disbanded and people re-allocated to other groups which delayed two groups settling.

Each cell has a leader and apprentice leader. This means the group is able to multiply through a combination of evangelism (we hope) and new youth moving in from the younger age group. It also helps us cope with the older youth who leave for university each year. However, it means that we are constantly releasing and training new leaders. The age range of apprentices and leaders is 14–20 though most are in the 16–18 age bracket. Our youngest apprentice is just 14 and seems to be coping very well in that role.

Small group leaders and apprentices come together with Andrew and myself each month for training to: evaluate where groups are in relation to the values; look at what needs to be adjusted as a result of that; learn new leadership skills and build on existing ones; pray for one another.

In addition, we have launched each new academic year with a weekend where we bring all the youth together and work on our shared vision, val-ues and group dynamics. This year, in September 2000, this is going to take place on a regional basis for the first time.

Values

True to cell church, values form the basis for everything. Our values are every member ministry, every member maturity, Jesus at the centre, sacrifi-cial love, multiplication, and community life based around openness and honesty. Quality of group life depends on the implementation of these val-ues, all of which support the vision of the wider church. Any programme plays a secondary role to the values. Most are developing well, though there is some hard work involved in growing community across the age range. There is a tendency to 'swerve to rot'—to veer off into comfort, habit, ease—so returning to the values at every review/training time is crucial.

Discipleship operates through a three year rolling teaching programme that focuses heavily on applying biblical teaching to individual and group lives through the work of the Holy Spirit. It is not traditional Bible study. Notes are written in three week blocks by ourselves and other individuals in the church who have teaching gifting and who we are training. We are also investigating using pastors in tailoring the notes to individual groups. We based the 'three year cycle' on YWAM's discipleship cycle. Notes are written around the classic four Ws of cell: Welcome—reforming the group at each time together; Worship—time to give thanks and worship together, not re-stricted to singing; Word—the Bible and its application to life, through ac-tivity, discussion and prayer, which results in a high level of individual accountability within each group; Witness—how does this affect our not-yet-Christian friends? What are we doing about them? Prayer for them.

We recognize that different components have changing emphasis as the group develops. Most of our small group notes and evaluations are winged around on email. We are currently exploring putting further notes on a website for those who want to follow things up. A sample of notes and an evaluation sheet are available from the author.

Pastoral Oversight

After the first 2 years it became apparent that we would be unable to pastor the group leaders to the extent that we felt they needed. We therefore introduced 'pastors' (cell supervisors)—adults who would be there prima-rily for the benefit of the group leaders, to support, encourage and help them handle any pastoral issues that arose. When new groups form we expect the pastor to be present in the small group every other week—not as a leader, but in order to be able to evaluate and review the leading of the group with the leader afterwards. This helps the group settle quickly and become fo-cused on the task in hand. In addition we meet with pastors once a month to pray for the leaders, review how things are going and work through any serious pastoral issues. With peer-led small groups now covering the 12+ age range, the role of pastor becomes crucial in helping and mentoring the leader and apprentice. They have not taken over and the group members do not defer to them. Pastors also help facilitate group socials/outreaches— serving the leaders in setting these up and making sure they happen.

Continuity is crucial in youth and children's work. At St Alkmund's, chil-dren's church takes place on a Sunday morning during the service. The chil-dren are in small groups down to the age of five, operating with the same set of values as the youth small groups, and coming together once a month for a celebration. I am looking at ways of developing leadership skills amongst the children. Outreach is more formally organized through events linked to festival times in the year, though we are planning to launch a weekly 'Kids

Klub'[12] later this year. The transition year (school year seven) has run in a new way this year, called 'ARK' because we aim to keep them safe through their first year at secondary school. It also aims at preparing them to move to peer-led small groups in September. We have got parents together to pray, discuss and outline the current vision and values and where we are going with their children in the future.

Gains and Losses

The most notable gain has been the growth and development in the young people. They spend time in prayer and preparation, and model that to others. Young leaders have been stretched, frustrated, excited and envisioned , as they have been given tasks beyond their strength and have had to rely on God to see them through. There has been an increased hunger and passion to see God act—the young people started and run early morning prayer meetings in several schools around the city, with a central cross-church one midweek. They show greater confidence to take part in their own meetings, but also in mixed age meetings, in every aspect, including ministering in the power of the Spirit. The openness and honesty within groups and the sense of greater accountability has resulted in increased commitment to daily discipleship. And there has been a releasing and recognition of gifting amongst those involved—preachers, pastors, teachers, evangelists.

On the other hand, evangelism has not developed as rapidly as we would have liked. There is still a 'two world' culture ingrained into some of our young people, though an increasing number of them are sharing our frustration. We are currently working on strategy that includes overseas outreach, and outreach in a town close to us as well as developing their ongoing friendship evangelism. Good friendships are forming, and some of the people on the fringe are making a definite commitment. We have also lost some youth— for some the cost was too high. This has happened in some instances where parental models have been in conflict with our vision. In others, where young people who have been brought to church through their childhood, are not Christians or do not want to have anything to do with it any more. Those we have to let go and trust God for.

My conclusion is that I would walk the same path again—and we are only a short way down it with much ahead at this stage. Our expectations of the youth have grown immensely, we have seen God be faithful in all the risks we have taken and seen his grace abound in all the mistakes we have made. Primarily that is not because of us as leaders, but because God is passionate about this generation. He has invested in them and is using them in ways that we would only have dreamed of five years ago.

---

12   For an account of this mission strategy, see Grove Evangelism booklet Ev 45.

4
'Big Bang' Transition at St Mark's, Haydock
Phil Pawley

I have chosen this story because it is perhaps applicable to the widest range of churches and parishes. It is the case of an existing church taking on the challenge of making the transition to a cell-based system. St Mark's is an example of a church committed to growth which on the one hand recognized that their home groups were tired and stale and on the other hand were aware of the need for a more discipleship-based approach to evangelism.

They opted for ceasing the old-model home groups and launching the new cells all at the same time—the so called 'big bang' approach. As a large church this required considerable leadership gifts in the management of change. Their hallmark has been flexibility and being appropriate in all the ongoing development as they have addressed the quality of cell life, adapted models for multiplication, are evolving children's cells and integrating classic cell oikos network evangelism with Alpha and central social gathering events. Among these adaptations they have stuck with classic cell applications of a) the four Ws in all cell meetings, b) using the word from Sunday sermons applied to life in the groups, c) developing lots of new leaders and apprentices with substantial support, and d) peer-led youth cells (as in Derby).

No mission strategy has ever been directly transferable from one location to another. At the heart of our learning about mission over the last three decades has been recognising the need for enculturation. Cell church is no different. St Mark's, like every other church, is unique. The way the cell church vision has unfolded at St Mark's may give insights to other middle- to large-sized churches, but each will need to adapt these for their own circumstances.

In the early days of cell in the UK, everyone we talked to said starting with a prototype cell was the best way to make the change. But in St Mark's in recent years everything done has been based on consensus and unity of purpose. It therefore seemed illogical to have part of the church implementing one set of values (cell values) whilst the rest were doing something else. We saw that the unity of the church could easily be undone with this twin track approach to transition. It seemed clear that 'Big Bang' was the way for us to go—everyone leaping off together. But for the whole church to change in one go required careful preparation—training leaders, envisioning the church members, developing realistic expectations, and of course helping the existing 15 home groups prepare for the transition, which for some meant closing down. Beyond this was the task of forming 33 new cell groups—a mammoth task for sure, and a delicate one at that! So how did it all start?

A Bit of History

Haydock is a south Lancashire urban village on the edge of St Helens, formerly a coal mining town with other heavy industry. St Helens has more recently been experiencing significant economic regeneration. Haydock has only limited light industry, being mainly residential within the lower to middle socio-economic range. The predominantly white working class history continues to influence the culture, but more recent housing developments have brought some wealth into the area. St Mark's parish population is some 12,000 people, about half of Haydock.

St Mark's reflects the middle band of Haydock's population—neither rich nor poor. Significant renovation of the church in the early 1990s required sacrificial giving by many, leading to a greater shared ownership of the vision. The church building is located on the high street of Haydock, and when fully refurbished in 1995 a café and a reception area were added to the front. It is a warm and welcoming building and an excellent facility not only for the church family activities but also for conferences.

The church currently has 41 cells with 350 participants. This is about 65% of the 550 regular Sunday attendees. During a recent 9 week long survey 950 different people attended at least one service in that period, including baptisms and memorial services. So like most Church of England urban churches, there is a sizeable fringe.

Normal Sunday attendance consists of two identical morning services, both of which are family-oriented and could be labelled 'mildly charismatic evangelical.' A total of 350 people attend these, with another 50–75 children in parallel children's church.

The 2.30pm service is more traditional and has a regular attendance of 35–50, and recently the evening service has been pruned to make way for a three-week cycle of training, fellowship and prayer events with an average attendance of 100–160 depending on what is on. Food features quite regularly, and the aim for the evenings is celebration, equipping, or outreach.

Changing to cell church by the 'Big Bang' method normally requires years of preparation. Phil Potter's ministry at St Mark's began in 1988 and throughout his early years he laid the foundations and values that are at the heart of the vision. The church embraced the work of the Holy Spirit and learnt to expect the presence of God as a normal part of life. Every member ministry was not just talked about but actively encouraged both within the services and home groups. Ministry Teams went to other churches and even as far as Africa. Servant leadership was modelled and a core leadership team made decisions and vision development a corporate activity. Practical application of truth, based on sound biblical teaching, brought discipleship to the heart of the church. A commitment to *Alpha* meant relational evangelism was the norm. All this laid the right foundations for the transition to cell church.

The Process of Transition

Be sure of the foundations. Having the foundational values of cell church already in place at St Mark's meant the process of transition itself was faster than might be expected. The core values of cell church were, nonetheless, systematically taught through Sunday sermons and other opportunities.

Share the vision with key leaders and then the whole church. St Mark's Core Leadership Team attended a cell church conference in North Wales in 1996. They embraced the vision and began planning and praying for the transition. The vision was shared with the wider leadership through PCC, and then with the whole church through Sunday preaching series, church magazine and other means throughout 1997. Special vision and prayer evenings were also held.

Appoint and train cell leaders. By autumn 1997, St Mark's had run *Alpha* for about four years and had a pool of potential leaders to draw on. *Alpha* showed that plenty of people could lead small groups provided they were given adequate training and support. Cell picks up on that principle, so a comprehensive training programme for the potential cell leaders and co-leaders was run. Of the more than 50 who attended, 33 were asked to lead cells and the others to co-lead.

Form the cells. This was a difficult task, requiring much sensitivity, knowledge of the congregations, juggling, and a few other party tricks! People were allocated to a cell and when the lists were publicly displayed, they were invited to discuss any concerns with the leaders. Where possible, personal preferences were taken into consideration. Some cells were single-sex, whilst others reflected a particular age range. Most had a broad cross-section of the church. The object was to help people feel they belonged, and to feel comfortable in sharing their faith with others. The principle in forming cells seems to be 'Do whatever works.'

Youth and children's cells. Moving the youth ministry into a cell based model took a little longer, but has been worth the wait. After trying various styles, the youth cells are now led by teenagers with lots of help and support from adult youth leaders. Youth cells meet on Thursday night in the church hall and have a varied programme. Cells normally combine for a time of worship, followed by individual cell activities. This makes the most of young people's need for large 'tribal' gatherings, as well as small group intimacy.

The children's ministry has taken more time to adopt cell principles. Children meet in a similar manner to the youth, but only on Sundays. We are continuing to look into how to adapt our ministry to our children to reflect our commitment to the underlying principles of a cell church. Watch this space!

The four Ws. These could be: Work hard, Weep a lot, Whine a little, Wonder at God. To suggest that keeping 33 cells alive and kicking is easy is to deny reality! Initially the hardest cells to satisfy were those trying (or not trying, as the case may be) to make the transition from existing home groups. Changing from Bible study groups to applying simple truths to daily life meant quite a challenge to spiritual pride. Another problem encountered was getting the quantity of material for a cell meeting right. At one point the quantity nearly sank the ship.

Applied truth is the cell value relating to the 'Word,' and leaders are now provided with three questions based on the sermon each Sunday.

• What did you learn from this passage of Scripture?
• How does this apply for your life?
• How can we as a cell group help you to embrace this truth and put it into action?

Added to these, leaders are also provided with suggestions for their 'Welcome,' 'Worship' and 'Witness' components.

Pastoring the Leaders. Pastoring the pastors is essential with cell. Four initial training evenings are followed by regular and ongoing training and support. Initially leaders met monthly for two hours before a Sunday evening service. Training included reviewing the four Ws and developing a common resource of ideas for the Welcome, Worship and Witness components. Each cell leader and co-leader has a cell pastor who meets with him or her for prayer and support. The cell pastor has up to four cells to care for and visits each of these once a month. Recently the training meeting became bimonthly, with cell pastors meeting their leaders for a 'Cell Health Check' in the intervening month. No system is perfect, as no doubt this too will change as the vision grows and develops.

Staffing the Vision

The need for staff became apparent and in 1997 Phil Pawley joined the church with a view to working half time. He was appointed as Director of Mission in January 1998 to coincide with the launch of the cells. A curate, Will Cookson, was also appointed later that year, bringing the number of paid church staff to five—full-time Vicar and Curate, a half-time Director of Mission, a part-time Administrator and part-time Pastoral Care Co-ordinator. The addition of a Youth Pastor is currently being considered.

Growth and Multiplication

It was important to recognize that not all the new cells would make it through the first year, but although a cell may die, the people do not (well, not normally, anyway)! They are placed into other cells. It is also important to realize that simple multiplication is not the only way to grow. Sometimes it is more appropriate to reform several cells rather than wait for them all to grow large enough to multiply. Thus, careful co-ordination can allow two or three cells to become three or four. The net gain may only be one cell, but the reorganization that accompanies this process can give all concerned a change and a breath of fresh air. We have found that a slavish adherence to a purist approach can stop cells from growing and multiplying. The best rule of thumb is 'If it works—do it.' After all, who said the only way to multiply was wait until a single cell divides? Using this practical approach has helped St Mark's to grow from 33 to 41 cells in two years.

Developing an Evangelistic Process

To tell cells to 'go do evangelism' and yet to fail to provide them with special central events is to invite dissent and disaster. Cells operate best at the 'friend-making' end of the evangelism spectrum. The church provides regular events at the sowing and reaping end of the spectrum and an ongoing *Alpha* programme to which cell members can invite their friends.

The End of Phase One

In cell terms it is still early days. St Mark's began the process of transition in 1998, and the number of cells, and people participating in them has continued to grow. There is a clear sense in the life of the church that cell is at the heart of the vision. All leaders and people in ministry are expected to be in a cell group. Growth is not spectacular, but there is growth. In the 1990s St Mark's grew 100%. This, at the end of a decade of significant decline in the wider church, is good news indeed. Cell values have been at the heart of the growth. And more recently, the transition to cell-based ministry has quickened the growth. St Mark's presses on, with one goal in mind—to reveal God's glory to the nations.

5
Transitioning a Transplant—'Harvest', Margate
Kerry Thorpe

Our last story is unusual in combining planting and transition to cell church. So although a new church was planted by taking 50 from Holy Trinity, Margate, basing it on a cell system involved all the changes of ingrained values, expectations and attitudes of existing leaders and people from a home group background. Of the four stories, Kerry and Eunice are trying the most closely to follow 'pure cell' patterns with ongoing insights from Singapore. However, the honest account again highlights an evolutionary growing into classic cell structures and systems. It is also fascinating that the plant's authorization as a non-parochial, social network-based experiment, enforces the cells oikos *principle of evangelism as the only option. They are prevented from diluting this by adding normal parish programmes and visitation. All in all this pioneer venture offers every possibility of testing cell in evangelism and mission for many emerging 21st century contexts.*

'There has to be a better way of doing church.' *Harvest* was born out of twenty years of ministry experience during which the biblical idealism and personal longing that characterized my initial call was never quite eradicated by the harsh realities of ministry in a fallen world. I have spelled out the rationale behind my personal search for new wineskins of church life in *Doing Things Differently—Changing the Heart of the Church* (Grove Evangelism booklet Ev 40). In *Harvest* we now have the scope to explore how far the principles of cell church planting can be taken in an Anglican context.

Harvest is an Anglican cell church plant. We have no geography, no parish, no designated area. We are a network cell church. We meet for Sunday worship in Northdown Primary School, Margate. Through the week we meet in six adult cells and one teen cell. The children meet in age-specific groups alongside the worship on Sundays. We are currently a total of 64 adults and 42 children.

For five years I was Vicar of Holy Trinity Margate, in the Diocese of Canterbury. It was from the 'Family Congregation' of that church that our core planting team was drawn. It is in that parish that our Sunday venue is situated. Our Anglicanism is expressed through the increasingly appreciated Lambeth Quadrilateral of 1888: Bible, creeds, sacraments and episcopal oversight. I have a licence from the Archbishop, as a public preacher 'within the Diocese and jurisdiction of the Archbishop.' We are held accountable through a reference group chaired by the Archdeacon of Canterbury, to whom I make a written report three times a year, prior to our meetings.

For me, the discovery of cell church principles was not a new revelation. Rather it was the articulating of those biblical insights that had excited me most from the earliest days of my Christian life. These include the high value placed on relationship, the expectation of personal discipleship growth, accompanying a genuine release of ministries and gifts, a framework for consistent outreach and a refreshingly risky dependence on the Spirit of God over and above inherited church structures and expectations. As the original vision for cell church was taking shape, we explored the possibility of one entire congregation from within the family of three congregations that comprised Holy Trinity making the transition to cell church. That was not to be. Approval would only be given on condition that I lay down my role as Vicar and plant out with those who would immediately share the vision. So that is how it was.

Harvest was formally launched in September 1998. By that time we had laid a foundation of teaching on cell values. That was about it. Everything else we would have to learn as we went along. I did a lot of reading and went to enough conferences to gain an overall impression of what cell church was supposed to look like. It is just such a brilliant theory—compelling. We, however, were working with real people, with real differences, in the real world. As all this reality hit us, I began to notice, in the worldwide success stories, little snippets of reality that I had previously missed. Like the famous South Korean Pastor who was told by his people 'It'll never work here'! Like the Singaporean church where the leaders said, after five years, 'Oh, I think I see what you're getting at now'! Like the British cell church leader who said after five years, 'I now think the transition period is more like seven years'!

So now we have added to our visionary enthusiasm a realistic assessment of the size of the task. We have also come to appreciate the insights of those who have trodden this path ahead of us. There really are no shortcuts. We have already come to see that what matters is not the pace of change, but the fact of change. Here are some examples.

Cell Leader Support

When we started, we operated a system where I was responsible for every cell. Each cell leader met with me for a minimum of one hour per month, for a face to face appraisal, mentoring, discipling session. In addition there was, and still is, a monthly forum for all the leaders together. I would visit each cell as and when I could. I was running an *Alpha* course at the time and meeting weekly with a kind of Standing Committee of two so-called Wardens (nothing formal you understand because we have no parish, so no electoral roll, so no elections!) plus a Treasurer and a Secretary. After a year we recognized that this was not the best way. I understood for the first time the value of the cell coach role. The two Wardens became, with me, cell coaches. We each have two cells; we belong to them and attend regularly. We meet with each other and then with our respective leaders for the personal mentoring dimension. That is the heart of the cell system—one person discipling another, being accountable and having a soul friend, knowing that our growth matters as part of something bigger.

One-to-One Discipleship

It took eighteen months to initiate the one-to-one sponsoring strategy. Even then we introduced it to whole cells at a time. We used material from Singapore, *Beginning Your New Life* in the re-written Lawrence Khong version. The booklets are designed to be used, over six weeks, by an existing Christian with a new believer, in a one-to-one, one hour per week setting. We made it the subject matter of Sunday teaching, then gave booklets to everyone and had them mentoring each other, in twos and threes, in the cell setting. It has come on board slowly and in easily manageable steps, but it is happening! We now have two or three people who were introduced to the material in that setting, meeting with new believers in the classic one-to-one sponsoring role. We are getting there slowly.

Evangelism and Our First Cell Multiplication

Two years in, we are about to multiply our first cell. It started with five people. In our early days we were joined by a handful of people who were Christians but not attending worship anywhere locally. One or two people, on moving into the area heard about *Harvest* and joined. And a small number have actually come to faith through our own *Alpha* initiatives, sometimes run by a specific cell, sometimes run alongside the cell structure. One way or another, we are gently growing. So in this group at least, one becomes two. When it reached standing room only, the first sub-division happened naturally, with half the group meeting in the dining room and the other half in the lounge. Everyone came together for the initial worship time. That way, new leadership began to emerge, without the task seeming too big a step first time round. Developing new leaders is integral to future growth. We went through our first year wondering who the next generation of leaders would be. It is slow going, but when we have done it once, then further multiplications will seem more achievable, or so we hope!

The Challenge of Personal Change

Much the greatest challenge is working with people through their growth barriers. Most of us settle for less than our best. Most of our church structures allow us to do so, indeed collude with us in doing so. Cell is dependent on us growing in Jesus, breaking through the strongholds that have held us captive. When the vision for *Harvest* was first being held out, I was told more than once, 'It's a great vision but you could never do it, you don't have the relational skills.' I have had ministry for that and set aside the negative influence of those words! But it makes the point well. It has to start with me! Unless I can model some growth in a damaged area of my life then I cannot expect that kind of breakthrough in others. And it is so dependent on relationship. I have come to see that relationship is the heart of the gospel, both its message and its method.

So we need to be a church growing with God. We are also entirely dependent upon growing relationships with non-believing friends, because we have no parish, no permission to minister as *Harvest* into our community—that is the price of staying loyal Anglicans. But the cell system is proving its claim to free people up from church-based programs to develop new social contacts. Finally, and against that background, it needs to be said that we work hard at, and contribute visibly into the life of the local churches, taking a leading role in the coming together of churches in Thanet. Our vision is a kingdom one, and not just our little experiment!

Editor's Postscript
Bob Hopkins

In my introduction I emphasized the significance of cell for today from the standpoint of mission principles, using three analytical frameworks. I also stressed the need for flexibility in adaptation to the context. In our four stories we have seen this work out in application of cells in non-book UPA, youth work, blue collar Merseyside and white collar Kent.

All the stories illustrate the fact that to adapt the principles appropriately, the emphasis must be on values not on structure. I sense many just look at the structure and are either put off by its complexity and jargon or get enthralled by it and loose their freedom to adapt it.

These stories also highlight the fact that cell values are in harmony with so much of our postmodern pluralist culture. The creation of real community meets the need for belonging and identity. The shift from head knowledge to application and experience echoes not only the words of Jesus but is also so appropriate to our culture. It may also offer the possibility of at last changing the lifestyle of Christians from the pervading and addictive aspect of our culture. The mission focus of the small group and engagement with the world meets the need for purpose and significance.

It should not surprise us that in so many parishes youth work is shifting to some sort of cell-based model. The young are at the forefront of our accelerating social change and so we should look for signs of the most significant lessons for evangelism and mission amongst them. But let us see these as real lessons for what is already upon most of us—not just confined to the youth department.

I would highlight that rapidly changing culture not only challenges the church to become mission-centred but urgently requires us to rediscover leadership as purpose plus empowerment in the process of change. To introduce cell church principles in any form requires courageous and highly competent management of change. So do not be fooled by the inclusion of the St Mark's Haydock story and think cell is mainly for large churches where it is easier. Quite the reverse. Most large churches we have worked with, despite recognizing their 10- to 20-year-old home groups are struck in a rut, have backed off the challenge to change as being too complex and subject to too much resistance.

But whether large or small, when any church creatively explores cell principles it should open up new and exciting landscapes for empowering people at many levels. At its best it embodies the paradox of stronger central leadership giving away far more responsibility, ministry and initiative.